From Past to Present:

A Guide to Interviewing Elders & Preserving Family History

Judy Helm Wright

Published by Artichoke Press

From Past to Present: A Guide to Interviewing Elders & Preserving Family History

Published By Artichoke Press

©2024 Judy Helm Wright—Author/

Personal Historian/IntuitiveWiseWoman

ISBN (Paperback): 979-8-9900840-0-1

eISBN (eBook): 979-8-9900840-1-8

For additional parenting, wellness, life story writing, end-of-life books, and programs, please see our websites:

https://www.ArtichokePress.com

https://www.MemoirLifeStoryWriting.com

Connect on social:

https://www.facebook.com/MemoirLifeStoryWriting

https://www.Instagram.com/judyhelmwright

https://www.youtube.com/c/JudyHelmWright

Medical Disclaimer: Please use this book as a guide and suggestion, not as medical or psychological advice. Judy Helm Wright is not a doctor, licensed counselor, or professional consultant. She is a best-selling author, Certified Personal and Oral Historian, and Intuitive Wise Woman. If you are concerned about some aspect of your family's development or your mental health, do not hesitate to seek professional help.

J. H. Wright

This book is dedicated to Tara Gautney and Laura Pietkiewicz, both are able assistants, excellent editors, and proficient proofreaders. Thanks for keeping me on task.

Table of Contents

<u>Foreword</u>

I am honored to write a few words about my experience getting to know my parents. Oddly, one might think I did this while they were still living. Nothing could be further from the truth. While my parents were still alive, life seemed to get in the way of gathering those stories.

With the busyness of my career and my own children, history gathering seemed like a far-off project. Of course, I heard stories growing up, but they were in bits and pieces. Here and there, "tellings" and snippets of their lives. I never really heard stories with a beginning, middle, and end. Some may have been too hard to tell.

I did, however, get to know my parents much better after they had passed. My experience with getting to know my parents came through documents, letters, photographs, slides, and eight-millimeter film.

When my mother passed, 20 years after my father, I oversaw her estate. I had the challenge and the honor of going through everything in the home where they had lived for over 40 years. The house where I grew up.

In all honesty, it felt like a treasure hunt. With every box, drawer, and closet came more and more documents. I managed to fly them to California.

I took several years to look through them with intention, organize them chronologically into chapters, and hire a producer to create a ten-disc DVD memory project. I was so pleased with the results.

The production was made with moving music to match each chapter of my parent's lives as the images and photos scrolled across the screen.

I cannot stress how grateful I was to be able to have the time and the resources to do this memory project. It included my parents' childhood report cards, acceptance letters to colleges and universities, awards and accolades that my parents had received throughout their lives, and letters and cards received upon their deaths from precious friends and family.

There were also dozens of reels of film that my father had taken in the Korean War, along with numerous slides. Most memorable, however, were the love letters my father sent to my mother when he was stationed in Korea as a physician in a far-off MASH unit.

When my father was home on leave, my mother became pregnant with my oldest brother. His daily airmail letters were interspersed with declarations of love, hope, and desires for the future.

Anyone who is considering gathering the stories of their parents' lives should take this as encouragement to do so. Talk to your parents while they are still living. Discern the best questions to ask. Make a date to do it. Record their voices. I wish I had done all of that. At the same time, I am incredibly grateful for the unspoken stories yet documented in my memory project of my parents. Parents are such a treasure.

– S. Abigail McCarrel, LCSW, DCSW

Introduction

Hello from beautiful Montana, USA!

Thanks for buying this book and your interest in preserving the stories and oral histories of those you admire and honor.

Quick question: How many of you have bought or received those fill-in-the-blank journals for gathering life stories? I have three on my bookshelf right now!

The problem is most people *never fill them out*. The sheer number of questions and blank pages seems overwhelming.

"Where to begin? Does anyone care? What do my children's children really need to know? My story isn't that important."

Even though you and other family members have bought the beautiful journals and expected the grandparents to fill them out, they have not. Nor will they.

However, when a daughter or grandchild asks me to tell them a story of my parents, childhood, or ancestors, I am super enthused. One story leads to another.

The difference is the interested audience. I can see the attention of my listener, and I am available to answer any questions in real-time. This is a shared oral history.

Unless you are there to ask questions and guide the narrative, the stories and wisdom will be lost. This may be the most important work you ever do. It will certainly be the most spiritual.

Since blank lines are popular, we have included them too. But the difference is that you, as the interviewer, will most likely be writing in the spaces. You can leave this book for your subject, but chances are good, they will wait for you to ask the questions and record the answer.

Hence, _Past to Present: A Guide to Interviewing Elders and Preserving Family History_ is just what you need to help you document the stories you don't want to forget.

Have you felt a nudging of the spirit to capture the stories of the older people in your family before they pass or develop dementia?

You are being called to become the family historian. *You* will ensure that your older family member's names and stories are not forgotten. *You* will connect and gather the oral history of loved ones before it is too late.

Not only will you create a meaningful connection with your loved one, but they will also feel valued and cared for through your curiosity and interest in their lives.

My friend and mentor Richard Stone, M.S. author of *Stories-the Family Legacy-A Guide for Recollection and Sharing* said,

> *I have come to realize that each of us has a story to tell and that we all need to be heard. To die and not tell your story may be one of the biggest tragedies that can befall a person. If you let a person die without hearing his or her stories, it will leave a hole in your being that can never be completely filled (Stone)*

What is an Oral History?

An oral history is not the facts (such as births, marriages, and deaths) but the stories behind those events. Genealogy has many more facts, but we can find that information online. We need to hear firsthand the stories of the ancestors who shared, taught, and mentored.

Elderly folks have lived through and learned from their life experiences. Their wisdom and sage advice are powerful to younger generations who still face life's challenges.

A good oral history is more about the *how and why* rather than the what, where, and when. There will be other members of your family who enjoy genealogy, but you are putting the meat on the bones of information. You are capturing the stories and memories.

Most people who have lost a parent or grandparent wish they had the opportunity to listen to their stories and memories once more. If you take the time to ask questions and record a family oral history, even a very informal one around the dinner table, you will create a treasure for the future.

As you preserve your family's history, interviewing elderly members can provide invaluable insights and anecdotes. However, it can also be frustrating and inconvenient for the storyteller and the listener. Be patient and know you have been called to record this narrative.

I want you to succeed in this divine calling of being your family historian. Imagine the joy and knowledge your efforts will bring to future generations who read or listen to the stories you capture about your loved ones.

Testimonial from a Colleague and Class Participant:

I received this note in my mailbox (yes, he really did send it through the post office, stamp, and all):

> *For as long as I can remember, my family has asked my grandma to write her stories. But, of course, she never got around to it and said, "Oh, my life isn't that interesting. I just raised a family on my own after my husband was killed in a logging accident."*
>
> *But every holiday, we would ask her about how she coped with being left with five small children and no means of support. She would talk about deciding she*

didn't have time to grieve and started doing what she did best. Sewing and creating with materials on hand.

We all loved hearing her stories and talking about the quilts she had made for each of us and how she sold similar ones in the stores and made a living.

Of course, we didn't write them down or record them. Why would we? She would live forever, and we had years to collect the stories.

Then, all of a sudden, she was 97, and her eyesight was going. After taking your memoir class, I realized "if it was to be, it was up to me," and I got my phone and my hind end over there and started asking questions.

It was so simple to talk into my phone and then have it transcribed. My whole family will cherish this forever.

Thanks, Judy. I appreciate learning about the what and why we need to gather these stories before it is too late.

Your friend, John P.

Like John, I am betting that something similar has happened in your family or circle of friends. This is your sign that the time is now. Your children's children will be so grateful you took the time and effort to capture these stories. Everyone has a story to tell and wisdom to share.

The Three Deaths

I have written about this Mexican folktale in my "End-of-Life Stories" chapter, but it bears repeating here:

There are three deaths:

1. *The first is when the body ceases to function.*

2. *The second is when the body is consigned to the grave.*

3. *The third is that moment, sometime in the future when your name is spoken for the last time.*

Those last words have haunted me. Do you agree? I have gathered many end-of-life stories and know that many people are not afraid to die; they are afraid of being forgotten.

One of the ways we keep our names and the names of our family members on the lips of others is to share and gather our stories.

Why Write It Down or Record Stories?

The written and spoken word is a special legacy. Captured stories of those who have lived long lives will become a priceless memento of your family's heritage. It is a document that honors all your loved ones, both the storyteller and the story readers, for generations yet to come.

A story starts with a paragraph, a paragraph begins with a sentence, and a sentence grows from a word. Start with a question and then record the words, sentences, paragraphs, and stories of yourself and others.

Thank you for being so interested in finding and exploring your "roots" and compiling an oral and written history for your family's future generations. This may very well be the most spiritual work you will ever do.

Blessings and best wishes,

— Judy Helm Wright,
Author/Historian/IntuitiveWiseWoman

Please join us at www.MemoirLifeStoryWriting.com and www.ArtichokePress.com for additional books, online courses and free downloads.

I appreciate those who give me positive reviews on Goodreads or wherever you purchased your book. This gives me feedback and ideas for other offerings to assist you in "*finding the heart of the story in the journey of life.*" Thank you for your support!

Part 1: Preparing for Your Interview

I recognize you are busy and feel this project is falling on your shoulders. Been there, done that. However, the elderly are usually grateful that you want to visit and talk with them.

Preparing for your interview with your older family members is essential for creating a meaningful and productive conversation that respects their time, experiences, and preferences. This is an opportunity to capture your loved one's story and preserve your family history from their perspective.

Within these pages, you will find a comprehensive guide to effective interviewing methods, tools, and techniques to help you on your journey.

Through preparation and intention, you can create a supportive and respectful environment. This enables elders to share their stories with clarity, depth, and authenticity.

Chapter 1

Create a Comfortable Environment

When you and your loved one begin on your journey to capture your family history, it is important to establish a comfortable environment to hold your interviews.

When your interviewee feels at ease, they are more inclined to communicate openly, facilitating meaningful conversations and building trust. Effectively creating a welcoming and supportive atmosphere is essential to a successful interview with your elderly loved one.

You can begin by selecting a familiar and comfortable setting for the interview, such as your elder's home or a quiet, private space where they feel at ease.

Minimize distractions and ensure that the environment is conducive to relaxed conversation. This will help your interviewee feel reassured that this is a safe space, and you are a safe person to share with.

Respect the elder's personal space and preferences by allowing them to choose where to sit and ensuring adequate comfort and privacy during the interview. Consider seating arrangements, lighting, and temperature to enhance their comfort.

Take time to establish rapport with your subject before diving into the interview. Engage in casual conversation, express genuine interest in their well-being, and build a connection based on mutual respect and trust.

Approach the subject with warmth, kindness, and empathy, creating a welcoming atmosphere and encouraging them to share their stories.

Offer refreshments such as water, tea, or snacks to make them feel comfortable and cared for during the interview. This simple gesture can help create a relaxed and hospitable environment.

Use gentle and non-threatening body language to convey openness and receptiveness. For example, avoid crossing your arms, leaning in too closely, or exhibiting gestures that may appear intimidating or confrontational. Smile, maintain eye contact, and convey genuine interest in their experiences.

Foster a supportive and non-judgmental atmosphere where they feel free to express themselves without fear of criticism or ridicule. Listen attentively, validate their experiences, and offer encouragement and reassurance as needed.

Allow plenty of time during the interview to ensure the elder feels relaxed and unhurried. Avoid scheduling the interview during times of stress or fatigue. Be flexible with the duration of the conversation based on their needs and preferences.

Get feedback from a caregiver or spouse on energy cycles and appointments. Do they have more energy in the morning or the afternoon? Your interviewee may not be up to performing, even if they love the idea. If needed, break the interview into short segments.

Be patient and understanding if the elder requires extra time or assistance during the interview. Allow them to communicate at their own pace and be sensitive to any physical limitations or cognitive challenges they may have.

Ask if your loved one has any auditory issues before beginning your interview. Enunciate clearly when asking a question. It is also helpful if they can see your mouth to aid in lip reading.

Creating a comfortable interview environment for your family members sets the stage for meaningful and authentic conversations that honor their experiences, perspectives, and contributions to your family history.

<u>Notes to Self:</u>

Chapter 2

Be Flexible: Respecting Pace and Emotions

At the beginning of the interview process with your loved one, it is important to establish a supportive and empathetic environment. This allows them to share their stories comfortably and authentically.

Recognize that discussing past experiences, particularly significant or emotional events, may evoke strong emotions in your elderly family members. Respect their emotional boundaries by allowing them to express their feelings openly without pressure or judgment.

Refrain from challenging if they say something that you think is not true. Your subject will shut down if you raise your eyebrows or say something negative.

- **Personal note**: When interviewing my 96-year-old aunt, we agreed she would tell stories of her grandparents. However, she immediately started telling me a very personal story of her husband's abuse by a Catholic priest when he was a child. I listened to and recorded the story. Per my aunt's request, I only shared it with one female cousin and allowed her to decide how to reveal it to her siblings.

Practice active listening with empathy, demonstrating genuine interest in your loved one's stories and validating their emotions. Offer words of understanding and support, acknowledging the significance of their experiences and the impact it had on their life.

Foster a safe and non-judgmental space where your elderly family member feels comfortable sharing their thoughts, feelings, and memories. Assure them that their emotions are valid and that they have control over the pace and direction of the conversation.

Be patient and allow elderly family members ample time to reflect on questions and gather their thoughts before responding. Avoid rushing or interrupting them, give them space to articulate their memories and experiences in their own words.

Often, elderly people need a minute or two of silence to bring up a memory or answer a question. Recognize that memory is not always precise. Some memory loss is a normal part of aging.

Using the five senses to ask questions will help them remember moments in time with better clarity. You could say something like: "What did your family wear for holiday dinners with the extended family? What smells do you remember? What was your favorite dish? Who was usually there for the holidays?"

Pay attention to nonverbal cues such as body language, facial expressions, and tone of voice, which can provide valuable insights into the elder's emotional state.

Respond sensitively to their cues, offering support and encouragement as needed. When disclosing a painful memory, the interviewee will often hold their hands over their heart.

Approach sensitive topics carefully, recognizing that certain subjects may be difficult or painful for your interviewee to discuss. Allow them to decide whether they feel comfortable addressing these topics and respect their decision if they choose not to.

If tears or emotions arise, you do not need to say, "I know how you feel." Have a box of tissues nearby and sit quietly until your loved one indicates they are ready to move forward.

Validate your elder's feelings and experiences, acknowledging the significance of their stories and the impact they've had on their life and the lives of others. Offer reassurance and support, emphasizing their memories and emotions are valued and respected.

Respect your family member's privacy by maintaining confidentiality and discretion regarding sensitive or personal information shared during the interview. Avoid sharing conversation details without explicit consent and ensure that any recordings or documentation are stored securely.

Allow your elder to lead the conversation and dictate the pace of the interview, following their cues and adapting to their comfort level. Be flexible and responsive to their needs and preferences, prioritizing their emotional well-being. If you notice that a particular topic is causing distress, gently steer the conversation differently.

Explore positive and uplifting memories. Celebrate achievements, joyful events, and moments that bring happiness.

Express gratitude to the subject for sharing their stories and emotions, acknowledging the courage and vulnerability it takes to revisit past experiences. Thank them for their time, insights, and contributions to preserving family history.

Be sure to always end each interview session on a positive note. Please bring them back to the present moment and focus on the future. This is a great place to ask them what they would have for supper and their favorite meal.

- **Personal note:** I found that the most amazing end-of-life stories came as I was at the door, ready to leave. I would thank them for meeting with me and then say, "Is there anything else you want to share?" There always was.

Respect the pace and emotions of your elderly family member throughout the interview process. This creates an empathetic environment that honors their experiences, validates their feelings, and facilitates authentic storytelling. This approach fosters trust, connection, and mutual respect, enriching the interview experience for you and your loved one.

Notes to Self:

Chapter 3

Audio and Video Recording

Utilizing audio and video recording during interviews with elderly family members offers numerous benefits for capturing their stories and preserving family history.

Modern technology such as this can capture the interviewee's authentic voice, expressions, and mannerisms. This authenticity adds depth and richness to the storytelling, making it more engaging and relatable for future generations.

Furthermore, recording interviews ensures that no details or nuances are lost over time. It provides a comprehensive conversation record, including tone, emotion, and storytelling style, which may be difficult to capture through written notes alone.

Video recordings provide visual context, allowing viewers to see the interviewee's surroundings, facial expressions, and gestures. This additional layer of information enhances understanding and empathy, especially when discussing personal or emotional topics.

Nonverbal cues such as body language, facial expressions, and gestures convey important messages during interviews. Video recordings capture these cues, providing a more complete picture of the interviewee's thoughts and emotions.

Audio and video recordings serve as tangible documentation of family history. They can be archived, shared, and passed down through generations, ensuring that the stories and memories of elderly family members are preserved for posterity.

Recorded interviews can be accessible to family members who may not have been present during the original conversation. They can be easily shared with relatives near and far, fostering a sense unity and intergenerational connections within the family.

Reviewing recorded interviews allows for reflection and analysis of the content. Family members can revisit conversations, uncover new insights, and identify themes or patterns that may not have been apparent during the initial interview.

As a valuable educational resource, recorded interviews provide firsthand accounts for future generations of historical events, cultural practices, and personal experiences, offering a unique perspective on the past.

Helpful Tips to Use While Filming or Recording:

When video recording, ensure the camera is directed at the person being interviewed. Ensure you have tested all the equipment before the interview. This is vital.

- **Personal note:** One time, I did not check my equipment before starting my interview and realized later that the recorder did not work. My credibility was damaged, and some of the stories were different the second time.

If geographical distance is a barrier, conduct virtual interviews through video calls or recording software. Leverage technology to bridge gaps and facilitate meaningful conversations.

You may need to mail them instructions for using a Zoom meeting. Check into HelloAudio.com to capture snippets of history from family members worldwide.

I have added an informative chapter from my friend Amy Herrick's upcoming book. She has permitted me to share this with you.

Dictation is Not Dead!!

We are all so used to grabbing our cell phones and typing with our thumbs or using our keypads on our computers that we have forgotten how amazingly fast and valuable dictating our thoughts can be.

Using the new text-to-voice model for this old concept saves you tons of time by using the power of your voice instead of the power of your fingers.

Let this sink in:

- Your voice-to-text 24/7/365 virtual assistant (VA) is portable and travels with you everywhere.

- Your voice-to-text 24/7/365 VA is efficient.

- Your voice-to-text 24/7/365 VA is free to engage as little or as much as you want without adding another monthly or annual fee.

- Your voice-to-text 24/7/365 VA is faster than you are.

- Your voice-to-text 24/7/365 VA is not perfect, so proofreading is needed.

Have you ever timed how long it takes to type out responses on your cell phone? It will be much longer than you think. I will not even bring up when spellchecker "helps" you…

You already have options you could and should be using at your fingertips. Let us go over a few examples where you can evaluate this idea right now with the resources already at your fingertips, even if they have been underused until today:

On my iPhone, I can go to Notes, tap the screen, and tap the microphone at the bottom right-hand corner to activate talk-to-text. I have learned to hit the space bar between thoughts or paragraphs as I go because it cannot do that for me. Copy, paste, and email to me. **Free!**

On my iPhone, I can go to email, tap the screen, and at the bottom right-hand corner, I can tap the microphone, and I get to talk-to-text activated. I have learned to hit the space bar between thoughts or paragraphs as I go because it cannot do that for me. **Free!**

I can record a video on my iPhone and send it off for transcription, which is another option. May or may not be free.

On Microsoft Word, go to the home tab, look on the right and there is a microphone here too! I have been dictating much of the content you see here because it is so much faster than me typing it. **Free***!*

Google Docs' built-in voice typing feature converts your speech into text. Open a Google Docs document, go to "Tools" in the top menu, and select "Voice typing" from the dropdown.

Click on the microphone icon that appears and start speaking. Your speech will be transcribed into the document in real-time. Free when you already pay for this feature.

Are you a Zoom user? Start a Zoom meeting and enable cloud or local recording during the meeting. Conduct your meeting as usual, with participants speaking. After the meeting, Zoom will process the recording, which will be available to view/download.

To transcribe the meeting, you can use various transcription services or tools to convert the audio in the recording to text.

Some transcription services allow you to upload the Zoom recording for transcription directly, making the process more streamlined. May or may not be free integrations.

Microsoft Dictate is an add-on for Microsoft Office products, including Word, Outlook, and PowerPoint, which allows you to use voice-to-text functionality.

It utilizes the power of Microsoft's speech recognition technology. To use it, you must install the "Dictate" add-on from the Microsoft Office Store. Free if you already have this software installed!

Apple Dictation (Mac): If you have a Mac computer, you can use Apple's built-in Dictation feature. Go to System Preferences > Keyboard > Dictation and turn on Dictation.

Press the designated shortcut (by default, it is pressing the Function (fn) key twice) to activate dictation in any text field.

Do you use Searchie? There is a transcription processing option here, too, included in your fees.

Online Voice-to-Text Tools: Various online voice-to-text tools that do not require any software installation are available. Examples include Speechnotes, Online Dictation, and SpeechTexter, among others.

Open the website, allow access to your microphone, and start speaking. The tool will transcribe your speech into text.

This is the beginning of voice-to-text! How many of these tools do you have access to now? How many are you using daily? "Oh Amy, come on, use it for what?"

Brain flashes! You are in the middle of doing something, and you do not want to stop this project. I use my phone to dictate it; it will go to email, and I can find it later.

You need to compose a letter on the run, excellent, dictate it. Are you trying to draft an article or blog? Need to share a recipe? Do you want to dictate the steps as you do a step-by-step project to train someone else remotely? Did you see something that gave you an idea you wanted to remember? A book? Voice-to-text.

Give staff or family members detailed instructions on how to manage an emergency. Are you sick of replying about how you are doing when you or a loved one is sick? Dictate it once, then copy and paste it when kindhearted people ask. Edit as needed on what you share with whom.

I have families that successfully used dictation services to record priceless oral family history they wanted to share, but it would die with them if it did not get recorded.

We had Dad talk into a tool. All he had to do was to tell stories when he thought of one. When he dictated the story in a speech-to-text note, they were typed and they were sent to his daughter by email. She edited and compiled them all.

He could dictate anytime he wanted. The value of these stories to the family was priceless. It was inexpensive to get the result they wanted. It was an uncomplicated way to make it happen for everyone.

How could you leverage dictations to increase your profitability?

Dictations are not dead; they are repackaged as voice-to-text options that are dramatically underused.

Starting today, let us supercharge your productivity by integrating voice-to-text on at least three projects, and soon, you, too, will be speaking more and typing less.

If you save a mere 30 minutes a day, five days a week, for 10 years in dictating versus typing, you will have another 7,800 minutes a year to do something else. Amazing! That is 78,000 minutes or 1,300 hours in 10 years you do not need to type your thoughts.

Amy Rose Herrick, ChFC

America's Profit Building Specialist

785-224-8954

Notes to Self:

Chapter 4

Ask Open-Ended Questions

Asking open-ended questions during interviews with elderly family members is essential for fostering meaningful conversations and eliciting detailed, reflective responses. It is a valuable tactic for several reasons.

For example, an open-ended question cannot be answered by one word or phrase. You are looking for a more expanded answer.

Such a flexible strategy can invite elders to share stories, memories, and experiences in their own words. This helps capture a more personalized account of their lives.

Using open-ended questions prompt deeper reflection, allowing your loved one to contemplate and express their thoughts on various aspects of their lives, including relationships, challenges, and achievements.

Begin with questions that invite expansive responses, such as: "Can you share a memorable story from your childhood? What do you remember about your grandparents? How did you meet your spouse? What is your favorite time of the year and why?"

By avoiding yes or no answers, open-ended questions encourage the expression of emotions. Your interviewee can delve into the emotional nuances of their experiences, providing a more authentic portrayal of their journey.

Never ask a question that can be answered with a quick yes or no. If they answer that way, be ready to say, "Can you tell me more about that?"

Preserve unique perspectives by asking open-ended questions. This allows your family member to express their unique viewpoints, opinions, and personal insights.

This diversity of perspectives enriches the family narrative and ensures a comprehensive understanding of their lives. Being open and accepting of the stories they share will reveal your loved ones' unique character, personality, and wisdom.

When elders are allowed to elaborate, it fosters a sense of engagement and active participation. This can enhance the quality of the conversation and make the interview process more enjoyable for them.

Open-ended questions also provide the flexibility to explore a wide range of topics. This approach ensures that interviews cover diverse aspects of your family member's life.

In addition, this type of question respects the autonomy of your interviewee, allowing them to steer the conversation based on their comfort and priorities. It empowers them to share what matters most to them.

If your loved one expresses tears or anger, do not shut them down. These powerful emotions may have been hidden for many years.

If they tell you something that is hard for them to talk about, reassure them that they will have the final decision on whether it will stay in the story.

Your family member might share unexpected insights or stories when given the freedom to respond openly. This spontaneity can lead to discoveries that may not emerge through structured or closed questioning.

Encourage storytelling by allowing the interviewee to express themselves freely. Do not interrupt; allow the interview to flow.

Perhaps your interviewee wants to return to a story they told before. You can edit or add to it later. Just nodding or smiling encourages the person being interviewed to expand or continue.

Some Quick Tips:

- Print out your questions and let the subject see them in advance. Leave ample space between the typed questions so you can both take notes on your pages.

- Don't worry about specific details like dates or places. You can typically verify those later. You are looking for thoughts and feelings.

- If you can get names, it will help to do research online later on.

Asking open-ended questions is a foundational technique for conducting meaningful interviews with your elderly family members. It not only captures the richness of their stories but also respects their autonomy, promotes reflection, and strengthens the intergenerational connection within the family.

Notes to Self:

Chapter 5

Thematic Prompts

Thematic prompts will help you structure your interview with your elderly family member. They provide a framework for interviews, ensuring a more organized and comprehensive exploration of your loved one's life.

Think of the stories you will collect from your loved one as a string of pearls. The string is the theme, and each pearl is a short anecdote or memory.

You may include the entire "string" as a complete life narrative. Or focus on specific "pearls" concerning an era, philosophy, or event in more detail.

Start with broad themes such as childhood, family, work, and personal values. Then, pose questions related to these themes such as favorite childhood memories, career highlights, significant life events, lessons learned, and core beliefs.

Most people can remember their parents and their parents' parents. These stories will add to the fabric of the family history. Gradually delve into specific details, allowing the conversation to unfold naturally.

If your subject jumps around or gets things mixed up, bring them gently back to the original theme.

However, if the conversation takes a small detour, let it. You may get an even better story than the one you were expecting. It is easier to interview with one central area of interest.

Perhaps it was life on the farm, their first job, where their ancestors came from, etc.

- **Remember:** Never embarrass your family members or demean their story. If necessary, you can make a notation when writing it down. Here is an example: "Grandpa said his father's name was Johann, but I think it was Thomas, according to the family Bible. Johann was an uncle on his mother's side who lived close to them in North Dakota."

By structuring your interviews around thematic prompts, you will encourage the sharing of diverse and meaningful experiences.

Notes to Self:

Chapter 6

Crafting a Narrative

Crafting a narrative around your interviews with your elderly family members involves weaving together their stories, memories, and experiences. This will blend into a cohesive and meaningful story that captures the essence of their lives and the broader family legacy.

Begin crafting a narrative by identifying overarching themes and key events central to the elder's life story and family history. These may include significant milestones, life-changing experiences, cultural traditions, or personal achievements.

Develop a framework or structure for organizing the elder's stories and memories into a cohesive narrative. This could involve arranging the interview around specific themes or chronological periods, allowing for a logical progression of events.

Draw out personal insights, reflections, and lessons learned from the elder's experiences. Encourage them to share their wisdom, values, and perspectives on life, family, and community, adding depth and richness to the narrative.

Incorporate anecdotes, details, and vivid descriptions that bring the elder's stories to life. Paint a vivid picture of the people, places, and events that have shaped their lives, creating a sense of immediacy and authenticity.

Explore the emotional landscape of the elder's experiences, capturing their emotions throughout the life journey.

Highlight significant relationships, both within the family and beyond, and the impact they've had on the elder's life.

Provide context for the elder's stories by exploring the historical, cultural, and social factors influencing their experiences.

Help your audience understand the broader context in which the elder's life unfolded, deepening their appreciation for the narrative.

Incorporate perspectives from multiple generations of the family to create a multi-dimensional narrative that reflects the diverse experiences and perspectives within the family. Highlight the interconnectedness of family members across time and space.

Showcase moments of resilience, strength, and perseverance in the elder's life-story, demonstrating their ability to overcome challenges and adversity. Celebrate their accomplishments and the lessons learned from facing life's obstacles.

- **Personal note**: The very best life stories and memoirs are about overcoming staggering traumas or trials. Think of Frank McCourt's *Angelas's Ashes* or Joan Didion's *The Year of Magical Thinking*. By the way, should you consider yourself too old to be preserving these stories, Frank McCourt was 66, Joan Didion was 71, and I am 79 when writing these books. You are never too old to capture life stories!

Respect the individual voices and perspectives of each family member interviewed, allowing them to contribute their unique stories and memories to the narrative. Ensure that all voices are heard and valued in the storytelling process.

Celebrate family traditions, rituals, and customs passed down through generations, highlighting their significance in preserving cultural heritage and fostering a sense of belonging within the family.

Encourage your subject (and yourself) to impart the wisdom they have gained through experience. Be open about the lessons that have shaped them and the triumphs that fueled their resilience.

These insights can serve as a guiding light for your descendants.

By crafting a narrative that honors the elder's life story and family history, you create a legacy that preserves their memories, values, and experiences for future generations.

<u>Notes to Self:</u>

Chapter 7

Mementos, Collections & Memory Triggers

Utilizing mementos, collections, and items as memory triggers during your interviews is a powerful method to evoke detailed and personal recollections.

Bring some items to your interview that will remind the subject of memories related to your theme. Perhaps a small flag or ship to represent ancestors migrating to another country.

Using physical items can be a fruitful approach to interviewing your loved one.

Mementos and items often carry sentimental value and serve as tangible connections to specific moments in the past. They trigger memories associated with significant events foster a more vivid and detailed recollection.

The use of objects your subject might recognize engages visual and sensory cues, enhancing the interview experience. The sight, touch, and even scent of certain items can evoke memories and create a more immersive storytelling environment.

Incorporating items of personal significance demonstrates a thoughtful and personalized approach to the interview. It shows respect for your elder's experiences and allows them to guide the conversation based on their meaningful possessions.

Mementos and collections often hold stories that might otherwise be forgotten. Exploring these items reveals narratives about family traditions, milestones, and the evolution of personal tastes and preferences.

Whether it is a cherished photograph, a piece of jewelry, or a collection, these items become storytelling prompts that lead to more detailed recollections.

- **Personal note:** I gathered many stories from my mother before she passed. We used memory exercises to visit her home and possessions with her eyes closed using her imagination. She was able to tell me what she wanted to give to each grandchild and why. After her death, the grandkids said that they did not necessarily want the "things." However, the stories about the things and why she chose particular items for each grandchild were priceless.

Some items may have been passed down through generations. Discussing these heirlooms provides an opportunity to explore family lineage, traditions, and how possessions connect different family members across time.

Certain items have the power to transport individuals back in time. Using these memory triggers, you create an environment where your family members can relive moments from their past, tapping into a sense of nostalgia.

In the next chapter, I'll show you more about how photo albums can be used to evoke memories and the stories you'll want to pass onto future generations.

Collections often reflect personal interests and hobbies. Discussing these items allows you to explore your subject's passions, preferences, and the role these interests played in shaping their life.

Incorporating such items as memory triggers adds a multi-sensory dimension to the interview. This holistic experience engages various senses, making storytelling more immersive and memorable.

Using mementos, collections, and items as memory triggers enhances the interview by creating a personalized, sensory-rich experience. It facilitates storytelling and honors the tangible artifacts that hold a wealth of family history and personal memories.

<u>Notes to Self:</u>

Chapter 8

Photo Albums

Utilizing photo albums as a tool when interviewing elderly family members is a powerful approach that can enhance the interview process, evoke memories, and provide visual context to their stories.

Photo albums offer visual stimuli that can trigger memories and prompt detailed storytelling. As your interviewee flips through pages, each photograph becomes a potential gateway to a rich and detailed recollection.

They also provide a focal point for discussion, allowing your loved one to share stories of specific events, people, or places captured in the images.

A single photograph can remind your elder that everything seems perfect for a tiny moment in time, especially when looking at photos of fond memories. The rest of the story is what happens before and after the photograph.

For example, think of a picture of a young man graduating from college. What did it take for him to get to that moment? What were his hopes and dreams for the future? What transpired after his graduation?

Photo albums often follow a chronological order, facilitating a structured exploration of your family member's life journey.

Use the timeline provided by the photos to guide the interviewees through different phases and chapters of their lives.

Suppose your family member has memory difficulties and can't remember the subject in a photo; look for clues within the photo. For example, what year was the car made that they are standing next to?

Encourage your subject to narrate the stories behind each photograph. Whether it's a family gathering, a milestone event, or a cherished memory, these personal anecdotes contribute to a more personalized and intimate family history.

Photos can provide insights into the cultural and historical context of your loved one's life. Explore images that capture cultural traditions, historical landmarks, or significant societal changes, prompting discussions about the broader context of their experiences.

Analyzing photographs from different periods allows for discussions about changes in fashion, technology, and the physical environment. This exploration provides an opportunity to reflect on the passage of time and evolving societal norms.

Family members and friends are often featured in photos. Use these images to explore family relationships, roles, and dynamics. Discussing the people in the photographs can unveil valuable insights into your subject's connections and bonds.

Use the photos as a storyboard to outline your elder's life story visually. Arrange images chronologically or thematically to create a visual narrative that complements the spoken stories shared during the interview.

Photos often capture family traditions and rituals and albums often document significant family milestones such as weddings, graduations, anniversaries, and other important events.

Discussing these images can shed light on the significance of certain customs, reinforcing the importance of passing down traditions from one generation to the next. They can prompt reflections on achievements and the passage of time.

- **Personal note:** Keep in mind that memories can get clouded and confused by time. On my mother's video of her life, when we were going through photos, she pointed out a particular gentleman and said, "I think that might have been Uncle Jack, who was tall like that." Only years later, her younger sister Ruth said, "Oh, that wasn't Uncle Jack; that was the hired hand, and I took so many photos of him because I thought he was good-looking!"

Integrating photo albums into interviews with your elderly family members enhances the storytelling experience and adds a visual and emotional dimension to the family history.

Using these visual cues, you create a more comprehensive and complete story that captures the essence of your elder's life and legacy.

Notes to Self:

Chapter 9

Using a Family Tree

Creating and exploring a family tree is not merely an exercise in genealogy; it is a voyage into the heart of your family's history.

Each branch, each leaf represents a person, a life lived, and a story waiting to be discovered. Beyond the names and dates lies a wealth of narratives, anecdotes, and memories that can enrich your understanding of who you are and where you come from.

Using a family tree can be invaluable in gathering stories from relatives for several reasons.

A family tree serves as a visual representation of connections across the generations. As you gather the stories, you will uncover relatives you may never have known existed.

These discoveries can spark conversations with living relatives who can provide insights and firsthand accounts of those who came before them.

One of the most fascinating aspects of exploring a family tree is uncovering unexpected connections and stories. Perhaps you will discover a long-lost relative who played a significant role in history or learn of a family secret hidden for generations. These revelations can add intrigue and excitement to your journey of discovery.

- **Personal note**: This may be the most surprising part of your journey. You will have to decide how to include stepfamilies, common-law marriages, gender reassignment, abandonment, adoptions, and all the other relationships that occur in families.

So, how can you effectively use a family tree to gather stories from relatives?

Start by creating a visual representation of your family tree using online genealogy websites or software.

Reach out to living relatives to gather information, anecdotes, and photographs related to family members both past and present.

Conduct interviews with older relatives to capture their memories and experiences, using audio or video recordings to preserve their stories for future generations.

Organize and document the stories you collect, weaving them into the branches of your family tree to create a comprehensive narrative of your family's history.

At the end of this chapter, I have included several simple family tree forms to help you get started. Once you start collecting stories, you will need to expand, but these forms will give you a great way to keep things organized at a glance.

By exploring your ancestry and engaging with relatives, you can uncover a treasure trove of tales waiting to be shared, preserved, and cherished for generations to come. Who knows what fascinating stories and unknown relatives you might uncover along the way!

Family Tree Biographical Data Forms

Relationship & Name	Birth D=Date P=Place	Marriage D=Date P=Place	Death D=Date P=Place	Burial D=Date P=Place
Husband (full name)	D: P:	D: P:	D: P:	D: P:
Husband's Father	D: P:	D: P:	D: P:	D: P:
Husband's Mother	D: P:	D: P:	D: P:	D: P:
Wife (full name)	D: P:	D: P:	D: P:	D: P:
Wife's Father	D: P:	D: P:	D: P:	D: P:
Wife's Mother	D: P:	D: P:	D: P:	D: P:

Child(ren) Name(s)	Birth D=Date P=Place	Marriage D=Date P=Place	Death D=Date P=Place	Burial D=Date P=Place
1st Child	D: P:	D: P:	D: P:	D: P:
2nd Child	D: P:	D: P:	D: P:	D: P:
3rd Child	D: P:	D: P:	D: P:	D: P:
4th Child	D: P:	D: P:	D: P:	D: P:
5th Child	D: P:	D: P:	D: P:	D: P:
6th Child	D: P:	D: P:	D: P:	D: P:

*Use additional copies of this chart for notating siblings from direct family and extended family

Grandparents Names	Birth D=Date P=Place	Marriage D=Date P=Place	Death D=Date P=Place	Burial D=Date P=Place
Husband's Paternal	D:	D:	D:	D:
	P:	P:	P:	P:
	D:	D:	D:	D:
	P:	P:	P:	P:
Husband's Maternal	D:	D:	D:	D:
	P:	P:	P:	P:
	D:	D:	D:	D:
	P:	P:	P:	P:
Wife's Paternal	D:	D:	D:	D:
	P:	P:	P:	P:
	D:	D:	D:	D:
	P:	P:	P:	P:
Wife's Maternal	D:	D:	D:	D:
	P:	P:	P:	P:
	D:	D:	D:	D:
	P:	P:	P:	P:

Notes to Self:

Chapter 10

Using a Genogram

A genogram is a visual representation of a person's family tree that goes beyond the traditional scope of genealogy. It is a diagram that depicts familial relationships, names, and dates but also includes essential information about medical and psychological histories.

Social workers or medical professionals often use this to analyze patterns of disease and addictions. Psychologists might use a genome to see the family dynamic to find where behavioral patterns develop in the individual.

This tool provides a comprehensive and insightful overview of the hereditary patterns of behavior, health conditions, and psychological factors carried in the DNA through generations within a family. This information is best learned from the family's elders.

However, your elder may share sensitive information about ancestors they heard their parents gossip about.

A genealogy chart can be double-checked by public information on the web. This is the kind of information that, while helpful, is often surprising to family members and kept as "family secrets."

- **Personal note:** In our family, my sister Liz was able to go back four generations and list illnesses and the causes of death of ancestors. Once again, this information was gleaned from listening to older family members gossiping and sharing stories. Our brother was furious that she noted he was an alcoholic in a long line of alcoholics. Which is more important, his anger or the warning to his nieces and nephews about the prevalence of alcoholism within the family?

Key Components of a Genogram:

Genograms include symbols and lines representing **familial relationships**, such as marriages, divorces, parent-child connections, stepchildren, adopted children, foster families, and common-law marriages.

You can print a sample genogram from the web, but you may want to compile your list of various family members and their relationships to you first.

It includes everyone who influenced your development by right of bloodline or association. This helps in illustrating the structure and dynamics of the family unit.

The genome is not meant strictly for family related by blood or marriage but can also be chosen family or associates. In our own family, each of our kids brought a friend home to live with us for a month, or years. We provided the "safe home."

Another distinctive feature of a genogram is its inclusion of **medical history** within a family.

It visually outlines hereditary health conditions, chronic illnesses, and other medical factors that may have a familial pattern. This aspect allows individuals to understand their genetic predispositions and sensitivities better.

Armed with the insights gained from a genogram, individuals can actively participate in their healthcare journey. They can work with healthcare providers to develop personalized care plans that consider genetic and environmental factors.

In addition to medical history, genograms capture psychological factors within the family. This can include mental health conditions, behavioral patterns, and emotional dynamics that may be passed down through generations.

- **Personal note:** My family genogram was full of alcoholism, diabetes, and depression. Armed with this information, we could share the warning signals with our children and have them include the genogram in their medical records.

Individuals can identify recurring themes or trends in their family's medical and psychological history by visualizing hereditary patterns. This awareness can be crucial for preventive healthcare measures and early intervention.

If you have ever been to a family reunion or large gathering and wished you had a whiteboard to try to figure out who was who, and what was what, you will see the value of this tool.

 A genogram presents a larger and more medically oriented view of individuals in your family tree, but is less interesting than the stories and history your family members can share. So, keep getting the stories!

Notes to Self:

Chapter 11

Interviewing Those with Dementia

Interviewing with an elderly relative facing dementia requires a compassionate touch that respects their unique perspective. Adapt your approach based on your relative's comfort level and cues.

Dementia is not a normal part of aging.

Dementia or Alzheimer's is a loss of cognitive functioning and behavioral abilities that interfere with a person's quality of life.

If a particular topic causes distress, gently steer the conversation in a different direction. Many practical tips and strategies are available to make the experience meaningful for both you and your loved one.

If the subject has short-term memory loss or dementia, bring items from their childhood: toys, plush animals, a teacup, a scented lotion, and a swatch of fabric.

If you are allowed, bring a puppy or therapy animal, which may help your interviewee to recall old family pets and keep them in a relaxed state of mind during the interview. The more you can use items that employ at least one of the five senses, the greater the chance of connection.

Give your relative ample time to respond, as processing information may take longer. Avoid rushing the conversation; let it flow naturally and at their pace. Use a warm and calm tone to convey a relaxed atmosphere.

Frame questions straightforwardly for easy understanding. Avoid complex language and ask one question at a time.

Allow your relative to guide the conversation and let them share what feels natural. Be attuned to their cues so that you can adjust your questions accordingly.

Acknowledge that individuals with dementia may create stories to fill memory gaps. Approach these narratives with understanding and use them as opportunities to explore imaginative aspects of their life.

Music can also be a helpful tool to assist with the recollection of old memories.

In a 2024 interview with Cori Vanchieri from the AARP, neuroscientist Julene Johnson explains that she *"shifted to researching cognitive neuroscience and aging after observing an older woman with dementia who suddenly started playing piano in an adult day center. Everyone in the room came to life and started moving, tapping their feet and dancing. I was struck by how impactful something as simple as someone playing a tune had on the whole room. That inspired me to better understand what it is about music that affects us."*

Johnson continues to explain that *"There's more to learn. The NIH (National Institute of Health) have just launched a five-year research project to accelerate studies on music and dementia"* (Vanchieri, 2024).

Interviewing your elderly relative with dementia is an opportunity to celebrate their life and preserve cherished memories.

By approaching the conversation with patience, empathy, and adaptability, you can create a meaningful connection. This connection transcends the challenges of memory loss, even when imaginative stories might be woven into the tapestry of their true life's narrative.

<u>Notes to Self:</u>

Chapter 12

Creating a Timeline

Creating a timeline when interviewing elderly family members serves as a structured framework for organizing and contextualizing their life experiences.

A timeline can be a helpful organizational strategy because it can provide a clear sequence of events, allowing your elder to recount their life journey in a systematic manner. This chronological approach helps the interviewer and the interviewee navigate through decades of memories more efficiently.

A timeline can place personal experiences within the broader context of historical events, societal changes, and family milestones, which enhances understanding. Your family members can reflect on how external factors influenced their decisions, perspectives, and opportunities at different stages of their lives.

It can serve as a memory aid, prompting elders to recall specific events, dates, and anecdotes from different periods of their lives. This structured approach stimulates memory retrieval and encourages more detailed storytelling.

Rather than a yearly mark, historians have found that most people remember in seven-year cycles or chunks of time. Memories are often grouped into childhood, adolescence, young adult, middle age, and retirement.

Keep in mind, men and women conceptualize time differently. My friend, colleague, and fellow author Diane Rooks explains it best in her book *Spinning Gold out of Straw: How Stories Heal*:

> *Our reasons for telling stories influence the stories we choose. The traditional reasons for telling stories differ for men and women, although both told their stories primarily in small family settings. Historically, men's stories have been to entertain, answer why questions, and record events. Women, on the other hand, have told stories to establish feelings of community, teach life's lessons, and serve as memorials to people and things gone by. My own grandfather introduced me to Brer Rabbit and Uncle Wiggly and described how the boll weevil ruined the cotton crop. My grandmother told me life stories about her mother, grandmother, and other family members (Rooks,2012).*

- **Personal note:** Several male participants in my memoir courses divided their lives into segments around cars, jobs, or dogs!

By mapping out significant life events on a timeline, you can ensure comprehensive coverage of your interviewee's life story. This helps identify gaps in the narrative and prompts follow-up questions to explore specific periods or events in more depth.

Whether created digitally or on paper, a timeline is a visual representation of your interviewee's life trajectory. Seeing events laid out sequentially can improve understanding and communication.

Timelines serve as valuable family history documentation, capturing generational transitions, achievements, and challenges. They become enduring records that can be shared with future generations, fostering a sense of continuity and connection to one's roots.

By collaboratively creating a timeline with your elderly family member, you're actively engaging in legacy building. This allows your loved one to reflect on their life's journey, share their wisdom, and impart valuable lessons to younger generations.

Reflecting on their life events within the framework of a timeline can be a meaningful and introspective process for elders. It offers an opportunity for self-reflection, gratitude, and closure as they review their life's achievements and milestones.

Susan Wittig Albert, author of *Writing from Life: Telling Your Soul's Story* shares this exercise:

> *Begin by writing down every place you have called home and the approximate dates you lived there.*
>
> *Annotate your list with as many identifying characteristics as you need to create a picture of it in your mind. Perhaps you will recall the address or how the house looked. This may take a while, and if you've lived in dozens of houses, you may not want to do it all at once.*
>
> *Perhaps you don't think of every house you lived as a home. If the word has a special meaning for you, take a moment before you make your list to define what you think it takes for a house (or apartment, tent, RV, or castle in England) to become a home (Albert, 1997).*

Using or creating a timeline during interviews with your elderly family members provides structure, context, and visual representation to their life stories.

It facilitates memory recall, encourages comprehensive storytelling, and fosters a deeper appreciation of personal and familial history.

Notes to Self:

Part 2: Gathering the Stories

Gathering stories through interviews with your elderly family members involves a layered approach to ensure a meaningful exploration of their life journey. This process includes preparing for the interview by establishing objectives, but also includes a deeper dive into stories that have shaped your loved one into the person they are today.

In the following chapters we will explore the who, what, where, when, and why experiences your loved one has had throughout their life. By incorporating these different aspects into your interview, you can capture and preserve your elder's stories, ensuring that their legacy and family history are documented with depth, authenticity, and respect.

Chapter 13

Discuss Hobbies & Interests

Discussing hobbies and interests during interviews with elderly family members is beneficial to capture a more complete and personal family history. They are an important part of your interview for multiple reasons.

Hobbies reflect a person's individuality. Discussing these interests allows you to understand your family member's unique identity beyond familial roles.

Hobbies often involve a continuous process of learning and personal growth. Exploring these aspects provides insights into your loved one's pursuit of knowledge and skills throughout life.

We often take our abilities for granted, so compliment them on a skill or talent you have recognized. Ask about why they choose a particular hobby or interest. Were they able to enjoy this hobby when they were young or only after retirement?

You might ask, "I have always admired how you finish a job and are not afraid to take on projects. How did you develop this skill?"

Hobbies are often intertwined with personal history. Whether it's a lifelong passion or a fleeting interest, delving into hobbies can uncover stories related to specific periods in their life. Ask leading questions about a specific interest. For instance, instead of saying, "So, you like to read about the Civil War?"

Phrase it so the family member will be encouraged to expand on the subject, such as in the following example.

"Mom told me you were an expert in some aspects of the Civil War. What made you interested in this? What was the most surprising thing you discovered that most people don't know?"

Engaging in hobbies contributes to emotional well-being. Discussing favorite activities can reveal sources of joy, satisfaction, and resilience, offering a more nuanced understanding of your interviewee's emotional experiences.

Many hobbies involve social interactions and community engagement. Learning about your family member's social circles and connections formed through shared interests adds a social dimension to the family narrative.

While familial roles are essential, hobbies provide a window into life beyond those roles. It helps family members appreciate the multifaceted nature of their relatives.

Discussing hobbies and interests during your interview with your elderly family member enhances the richness of the narrative. This will give you a deeper understanding of their life experiences, sources of joy, and the diverse aspects that contribute to their identity.

<u>Notes to Self:</u>

Chapter 14

Reflect on Historical Events

Reflecting on historical events during interviews with your elderly family members provides context to their life experiences, enriching your understanding of their journey.

Historical events shape the cultural landscape. Discussing these events gives insight into how societal changes influenced your family members' perspectives, values, and choices.

Research major events that would fall within the timeline of your loved one's life before your interview to help formulate relevant questions and secure dates.

Many elders have lived through significant times in the world's history. Reflecting on these events helps uncover personal stories and emotions and their impact on individual lives.

For instance, those who lived through the Great Depression have tales of neighbors sharing food, money, and gas rationing cards.

Understanding how historical events influenced family members allows for identifying legacies and lessons. Elders may share wisdom gained from navigating challenging times, providing valuable guidance for future generations.

Furthermore, reflecting on historical events fosters intergenerational connections. It helps younger family members appreciate their elders' struggles and triumphs, fostering a sense of continuity and shared history.

- **Personal note:** When our grandson was studying about the Vietnam War in school, he spent an evening with his grandpa talking about his experiences. Grandpa could share stories and emotions he hadn't previously shared with anyone. They discussed some painful memories and why Grandpa didn't want our grandson ever to glorify war. It was a deep bonding experience for the two of them.

Historical events can fade from collective memory over time. By discussing these events with your elderly family members, you actively contribute to preserving both personal and broader historical narratives.

Notes to Self:

Chapter 15

PhotoScribing

In the age of snapshots and digital albums, every photograph holds a unique story waiting to be told. I learned this technique from Dennis Ledux, a fellow Association of Personal Historians member. He developed this when many people were scrapbooking and wanted to add more than a caption.

PhotoScribing, also known as photojournalism or cameo narratives, is the art of weaving captivating stories around the moments frozen in time by a photograph. This method of storytelling goes beyond the mere act of describing an image. It involves delving into the context, emotions, and memories captured within the frame, transforming a visual moment into a rich and immersive narrative.

This is such a good way to capture a story from an elderly relative by having them focus on one picture at a time. Here are some steps to make your cameo narrative come to life:

1. **<u>Select Your Photo:</u>**

Choose a photo that resonates with you — a moment that holds sentimental value, triggers emotions or sparks curiosity.

2. **<u>Observe Details:</u>**

Examine the photo closely. Notice the expressions, surroundings, and any notable objects. These details will serve as the building blocks for the narrative.

3. <u>**Ask Questions:**</u>

Ask the subject the journalist's questions of who, what, where, when, and why. Paint a vivid picture of the surroundings. Provide details about the location, time of day, and any significant elements in the background.

4. <u>**Craft a Narrative:**</u>

Start crafting your narrative. The best stories have a beginning, middle, and ending. Describe the setting, introduce the players, and unravel the story behind the photos. Describe the emotions conveyed by the individuals in the photo. Emotions add depth to your narrative, whether it's joy, nostalgia, or contemplation.

- What might each person be thinking or feeling? This adds layers to your narrative.

- Engage your readers with descriptive language that appeals to the senses. Allow them to visualize the scene and immerse themselves in the story.

Here is an example of photo scribing to help get you started:

Our First Christmas as a Young Couple at Offutt AFB, Bellevue, Nebraska, USA

Dearest family,

I want to share a story with you and hope you will enjoy it and remember your parents and grandparents fondly.

In 1964, we were young, broke, and in love. I worked in a bank, considered suitable employment for an officer's wife. Dwain was a 2nd Lt. trying to figure out the politics of military life.

We married in the summer of 1964, and rented a cute little house in Bellevue with other Air Force families as neighbors.

Our tree was up and decorated in a living room corner where we had made bookcases from cinderblocks and pine boards we had painted. We had a redwood picnic table for our dining room. We found an old bench somewhere, painted it, and I made a pillow covering for it.

In other words, we were very typical newlyweds with more ideas than cash. So, we made an ironclad promise not to buy each other any presents. We had the ones our parents sent and our dog Gretchen to cuddle on Christmas Eve.

In those days, banks and stores were friendly and generous with their customers. They gave out metal piggy banks, calendars, tablets, pens, chocolates, bank bags, and gold-wrapped chocolate coins.

So, I did what any loving and clever wife would do. I got all the freebies in the community at the bank, drugstores, etc. I wrapped them up and put them under the tree. It looked like a mountain of gifts.

*Dwain walked in the door at 5:30 after the Christmas party in his squadron, took one look, and said, "Oh s***! I thought we weren't going to give each other anything this year!"*

I tried to explain that they were all free and not very important at all. He just took off, and I heard the car racing down the street.

The only stores open on Christmas Eve were the convenience stores and gas stations. He came home with a bag filled with candy bars, gum, magazines, an artificial rose, etc. He probably spent more than if he had gotten me a cashmere sweater.

We have long since eaten or discarded all the other stuff except the Bank of Bellevue zippered pouch that we used with our business "We're Nuts!!" and the calendar for 1965.

We used to take turns hiding it and gifting it on Christmas. But we can't remember where we hid it! Now we talk about it and remember what fun we had that Christmas Eve when he opened all the many "gifts."

I still giggle, just remembering how blessed and in love we were. It took so little to make us happy. It still does.

The following year, he was sent to Vietnam and had to report to San Francisco on Christmas Eve.

We didn't giggle that night; we were bawling 700 miles apart. Typical military, he did not ship out until December 27th.

For 59 years and counting, we have considered ourselves blessed and fortunate, no matter what we receive as gifts.

Of all our blessings, you are the best and biggest gift we could ever receive.

Thanks for being you,

Mom, Gram, and GramGram

PS: Please print this out and put it in with your Christmas decorations so you will be reminded every year about the importance of sharing experiences rather than expensive gifts.

Notes to Self:

Chapter 16

Siblings and Extended Family

When we are children, siblings are the family members that grow up with us. We stay up late with them and play hard all summer long with them. We make mistakes with them and get in trouble with them.

When we are young, many people spend more time with their siblings than anyone else. They are our partners in crime. They are also sometimes the same people that we lean on, clean up our messes, keep our secrets, and get us out of trouble. Sometimes we have to do the same for them in return.

Many of the memories you make when you are young with your siblings last for a very long time. Siblings are some of the most important people in a person's life. Other extended family members often provide a similar connection, such as cousins.

While interviewing an elderly family member, ask about their siblings and other extended relatives. You will be glad you did. It's a significant part of their story for many reasons.

Siblings and extended family members contribute to the broader family narrative. Learning about their lives helps preserve a more comprehensive and accurate family history.

Inquiring about siblings reveals insights into family dynamics, relationships, and shared experiences. It adds depth to the stories and provides context for understanding the elder's personal journey. Exploring these relationships helps bridge generational gaps.

Younger family members can better understand their heritage and connections to relatives who might not be present.

Siblings often play key roles in family traditions. Learning about shared customs, celebrations, and rituals involving extended family members adds cultural depth to the family narrative.

Ask about the responsibilities of each person's role within the family. Example questions might be, "What household chores did you share with your siblings? How did you learn how to cook, drive, clean, cut grass, etc.?"

Questions about other customs might include, "Where and why did your family gather for get-togethers? Do you remember occasions such as weddings, funerals, or celebrations where you met other extended family members?"

Extended family members may have stories that the elderly individual might not share spontaneously. Prompting discussions about cousins, aunts, uncles, and more can uncover hidden gems of family lore. These personal tales contribute to a more vibrant and detailed family history.

Elderly family members may be the primary source of information about their siblings and extended family. They may be able to offer a treasure trove of anecdotes and memories.

Collecting this information helps fill gaps in knowledge, especially when family members have dispersed.

If there has been a breakdown in the relationship between certain family members, treat this subject with deep respect and non-judgment. Allow them to feel their feelings without rushing to get the interview moving.

Family dynamics can provide unique perspectives and rich storytelling material. It can also be a minefield of emotions long buried. Be prepared to move on to another topic if your loved one is uncomfortable. They may be ready to share more on another day or time.

An excellent story starter is to ask them to describe a typical day for their mom or dad. Can they describe what their parents looked like? Did they inherit any traits from their parents?

In essence, asking about siblings and extended family members during interviews ensures a more holistic and inclusive representation of the family's history. This fosters a deeper appreciation for the interconnected web of relationships that shape familial identity.

Notes to Self:

Chapter 17

Recording Conversations During Gatherings

Collecting family stories at gatherings is a wonderful way to preserve and share your family's history. It fosters connection, helps pass down traditions, and allows generations to learn from each other's experiences.

Take advantage of family gatherings to record informal conversations. Spontaneous and heartfelt storytelling often occurs in relaxed and familial settings.

Start the recording by having each member introduce themselves so the listener can know who is speaking and their place in the family dynamic. Voices can blend in an audio recording, making it challenging to understand who is speaking. This can be troublesome when attempting to transcribe.

Keep in mind that background noise can ruin the sound quality. It is better to go into a quiet room and sit close together during the interview.

Even though you can record the joint interview on your phone or recording device, I have found that a video is better because then you can identify the face with the voice.

If the subject becomes shy, embarrassed, or reluctant to share, don't push. Perhaps you can revisit a tender subject later in the interview.

The most important thing I learned when interviewing a group of older siblings at a family reunion was to address each member by name and then repeat the answer, such as in the following example. "Aunt Mary, you remember your favorite breakfast was oatmeal with raisins when you lived on the farm. Uncle Mel, you enjoyed your mom's pancakes. Can you share why that memory still makes you smile?"

Sharing anecdotes and memories strengthens family bonds and creates a sense of identity and belonging. It's a meaningful way to capture and celebrate your family's unique narrative.

<u>Notes to Self:</u>

Chapter 18

Capturing Multigenerational Perspectives

Capturing multigenerational perspectives enriches the tapestry of family stories, offering a comprehensive view of your family's history. This approach enables you to facilitate dialogue between age groups while encouraging those of every generation to share their perspectives on shared events or family traditions.

Begin by gathering stories from the oldest generation. Their experiences provide a historical context and offer insights into earlier times.

Explore how family dynamics, traditions, and societal norms have evolved across generations. Chronicle significant life events, achievements, and challenges from each generation. This creates a comprehensive family timeline.

Discuss common values that have been passed down through generations. Understanding these values helps connect family members across time.

- **Personal note:** This can be a minefield if your family's values are not aligned. We had a loud argument erupt during a family dinner when a teenager tried to convert her redneck uncle to her very liberal stance on abortion. YIKES!

Acknowledge that each generation brings its own unique experiences and perspectives. Embrace diversity within the family story. Note the example above, and tread carefully. You will have to assume the role of narrator. Prompting questions can help draw out more detailed responses such as in this example. "Uncle Gene, can you share what you remember about the grandparents? Uncle Todd, can you add to this story?"

Do your best to avoid having one person dominate the conversation. Give them an alternative opportunity to speak further by saying, "Grandpa, that sounds so fascinating about your time in the Army. Can I talk to you later, get the details, and add it to the family history?"

If someone disagrees with what is being said, handle it with poise. "Uncle Ted, we all have a different perspective of events. Perhaps I can interview you separately, and you can share what you remember."

Below is a short anecdote I would like to share about how unique generational quirks can be passed down through families:

> *The bride in a newly married couple cut off the end of the ham before baking it. Her husband asked why. The wife responded that her mother always cut off the end of the ham, and that was the way it was supposed to be. Not accepting "the way it was supposed to be," the husband called his mother-in-law and asked why she cut off the end of the ham before baking. The response was that her mother cut off the end of the ham. More curious than ever, the husband called Grandma and asked her why she cut off the end of the ham. The answer was that she had a small oven, which was the only way to get the ham to fit.*

> *Grandma had a reason for cutting off the end of the ham. The next two generations did not. They blindly followed custom without rhyme or reason. It was "the way it was supposed to be."*

How many of your customs do you follow because you perceive them to be how they should be?

By actively involving all generations in your interview process, you create a holistic narrative that reflects your family's collective wisdom and unique shared history.

<u>Notes to Self:</u>

Chapter 19

Where Generations Meet: A Jar of Questions

Gifted to me by our granddaughters from a youth camp, the Jar of Questions is a simple yet powerful tool to encourage multigenerational conversation.

This jar filled with questions can bring family members closer together by exploring ancestral stories.

It is perfect to use while on long car rides, eating dinner, or during family nights. Each question is a doorway to understanding our family's past.

Create your own Jar of Questions:

1. Find a simple jar or box and have some fun decorating it with the family (this is a perfect activity for little ones).

2. You will find a list of questions at the end of this book. Use these questions to fill your jar. You can print these or write them out by hand. Be sure to leave some space between each question so they can be cut out into individual strips.

3. Place these paper strips into your jar and give them a good mix.

You are now ready to use your Jar of Questions!

The versatility of the Jar of Questions makes it perfect for any occasion. Whether you use it on a road trip, while eating a meal, or during a cozy evening at home, it sparks conversations that bridge generational divides.

With questions ranging from childhood memories to life-changing events, it uncovers the uniquely woven threads that compose the family tapestry.

This activity is a call to action, a gentle nudge to set aside distractions and engage in meaningful dialogue with those we hold dear.

We had fun having the grandkids pull a question, and then before we answered, we asked them to guess what we would say.

For younger family members, the jar offers a glimpse into the lives of their ancestors, connecting them to their roots. For older generations, it's a reminder to cherish and preserve their family heritage.

But above all, it's a testament to the power of family bonds that endure over time.

As keepers of the Jar, it has been fun to pick one and tell a life story while video chatting with our grandkids.

If we want to preserve the story for later inclusion in our memoirs, we can easily record the call through an app or set up a phone nearby to record a voice-to-text transcription.

So, grab your Jar of Questions next time you're with loved ones, in person or online, and let the magic unfold! Through shared stories and memories, you'll find the true essence of family — a timeless connection that transcends generations.

<u>Notes to Self:</u>

Chapter 20

End-of-Life Stories

As a dying person comes to terms with mortality and begins to prepare for death, they may use a life review to find closure and a sense of completion. Capturing these stories during your interview is a delicate yet profound way to preserve your loved one's legacy.

End-of-life stories are a meaningful way to allow individuals to reflect on their life's purpose, achievements, and impact on others. It's an opportunity to shape their legacy in their own words.

- **Personal note:** People were more willing to open up to me, a stranger because I believed whatever they said. After all, I could not stand in judgment as a family member might.

Elders often share valuable insights and life lessons gained through experience. Capturing these stories provides a repository of wisdom for future generations.

Discussing the end-of-life can provide a sense of closure and acceptance. It allows your loved one to express their feelings, share final thoughts, and perhaps reconcile with aspects of their past.

When someone can share their story, their pain level goes down, and dying is more effortless. A life review allows them to reframe unhappy times and ask for forgiveness or understanding.

This is an opportunity to acknowledge and celebrate the achievements and milestones, ensuring your family member's accomplishments are recognized and remembered. They provide a platform for expressing gratitude, love, and appreciation.

Family members can share their feelings, creating a meaningful exchange of emotions. Some may choose to discuss regrets or seek forgiveness. This open dialogue can be a cathartic experience, fostering understanding and emotional healing within the family.

Even when family members were estranged, they were ultimately grateful to receive the document and gain some understanding of the interviewee.

As you prepare to wrap up the interview or walk out the door (this is an effective technique for all interviews) ask, "As we end our interview, is there anything else you want me to know?"

The Three Deaths

I want to share with you a lesson that has stuck with me from a Mexican folklore tale about the afterlife.

There are three deaths:

1. *The first is when the body ceases to function.*

2. *The second is when the body is consigned to the grave.*

3. *The third is that moment, sometime in the future when your name is spoken for the last time.*

Those last words haunted me. Do they make you think about your own legacy and the heirloom you are creating?

I have gathered many end-of-life stories and know that many people are not afraid to die; they are afraid of being forgotten.

There is that point in the future — hopefully, far in the future, your name will never be mentioned again. The wisdom and experiences you have amassed will be lost unless you leave a record of who you are and what you want to share with those who follow.

I once contributed to an anthology of stories published by the Association of Personal Historians called *Their Words Are Going to Linger.* Isn't that what we wish for ourselves and our loved ones? We wish for our words and names to linger on throughout history.

Even though my mother's life story, *More Roses Than Thorns: A Reminiscence of the First 90 Years of Life,* has been shared with the whole family, it is not what later generations refer to in times of stress. The family has read, but forgotten, much of her life story.

However, much more popular and well-used are her cookbooks: *Grandma Helm's Kitchen Counseling: Instructions of Life, and Love,* and *Casseroles from the Kitchen of Eula Dee Turman Helm: Beloved Mother, Grandmother, Great-Grandmother, Neighbor, and Friend to All.*

Her name will continue to be spoken because friends, family, neighbors, and organizations use her recipes and remember her prune cake for funerals.

We published 500 copies of the recipe book and once word got out, we sold or gave away all of them. I still get requests from all over the world for copies of the book. Word has passed from friends or friends of friends. Yes, her words are going to linger.

There was a past without us, and there will be a future without us. It is a stark reminder to share our blessings and wishes for those who follow after us.

Only some people who receive your family history will appreciate it right now. It may very well lay in the bottom of a drawer or moving box for years. But as often happens, the teacher appears when the time is right.

Approaching this topic with sensitivity and empathy is crucial. It allows your loved one to share their narrative on their terms, giving them a sense of agency and closure as they reflect on their life's journey.

<u>Notes to Self:</u>

Chapter 21

Legacy Letter (Ethical Will)

In addition to collecting your family stories through interviews with your elderly loved ones, consider assisting them in creating their own legacy letter.

Below, I have included an excerpt from an article I authored in Blazing Trails, a newsletter from the Missoula Senior Center, explaining what a legacy letter is and why creating such a document is important.

> *A legacy letter, an ethical will, or a heritage letter is a heartfelt document crafted to communicate your values, life lessons, and personal stories to future generations.*

> *Unlike a traditional will that deals with material possessions, a legacy letter is a spiritual and emotional bequest. It's an intimate conversation from the heart, intended to guide and inspire your children, grandchildren, and beyond.*

> *Can you imagine the joy your family will feel to get not one more toy or electronic gift but an actual outpouring of blessings and sharing your heartfelt wishes? They may only realize what a treasure you have given them once you are no longer here. But I promise they will be so grateful you made an effort at some point in their lives.*

> *We often need to remember the profound impact our stories can have on future generations.*

Here's a guide on pouring your heart into crafting a legacy of love that will be cherished for years:

1. ***Reflect on Your Journey:*** *Begin by reflecting on your life journey. Consider the pivotal moments, the challenges you've overcome, and the lessons you've learned. This reflection is the foundation of your legacy letter, offering your descendants a glimpse into the person behind the words.*

2. ***Capture Family Stories:*** *Weave the fabric of your family's history into the letter. Share anecdotes and stories from the past — tales of resilience, laughter, and even the inevitable quirks that make your family unique. These stories are the threads that connect generations.*

3. ***Pass Down Values:*** *Take the time to articulate the values that have guided your life. Whether it's the importance of kindness, the strength found in unity, or the pursuit of knowledge, these principles serve as a compass for your descendants, helping them navigate the complexities of their own lives.*

4. ***Express Gratitude:*** *Express gratitude for the love and support you've received and acknowledge the contributions of those who came before you. Gratitude is a powerful force that fosters a sense of appreciation and connection among family members, even across time.*

   If you need to ask for forgiveness, do so. Set an example for those who follow after you to assume personal responsibility for life choices.

5. ***Share Life Lessons:*** *Impart the wisdom you've gained through experience. Share the lessons that shaped you, the mistakes that taught you, and the triumphs that fueled your resilience. Your insights can serve as a guiding light for generations to come.*

6. ***Conclude with Love:*** *Wrap up your letter with a heartfelt expression of love. Let your descendants know that your love for them is eternal, no matter the distance or time. This closing sentiment reinforces the enduring bond that transcends generations.*

7. ***Print Out Copies on Beautiful Paper:*** *Even if you choose to make a recording or video, have a transcript made to accompany the spoken word (Wright, 2024).*

Whoops! Here is something our generation forgets…kids under eighteen can no longer read cursive. You will have to have it written on a computer.

Thank you for realizing you and your elders have lived a life filled with wisdom and experiences. When you share the journey, you provide a roadmap for your children's children and all who have the privilege to read or hear it.

This is a timeless and beautiful way to bridge the gap between the past, present, and future.

Notes to Self:

<u>Part 3 – Putting the Pieces Together</u>

Capturing an elder's life story and family history through interviews involves weaving together various elements such as open-ended questions, discussions about hobbies and interests, exploration of end-of-life reflections, and the use of mementos as memory triggers.

By creating a welcoming atmosphere and encouraging storytelling, one can delve into the elder's experiences, emotions, and perspectives. Incorporating multigenerational perspectives, acknowledging family traditions, and respecting individual autonomy enriches the narrative, creating a comprehensive portrayal of their life journey.

Now that you have conducted your interviews and gathered your loved one's stories, it is time to put the pieces together. The following chapters will guide you through the process of proper documentation and filling in the gaps within your elder's narrative. We will also address legal concerns and potential pitfalls you may encounter along the way.

Each piece of the interview process contributes to a tapestry of memories. While it may feel overwhelming for you at this moment, remember that the steps you have taken to collect and preserve your elder's legacy will foster deeper connections within your family across many generations.

Chapter 22

Transcribe and Document

Transcribing and documenting the information you receive from your loved one during your interviews is one of the most essential steps when collecting their stories.

Transcriptions allow for easier sharing and dissemination within the family. It can be a reference point for family members wanting to revisit or pass down the stories.

Moreover, this type of documentation aids in capturing nuances, emotions, and details that might be missed during casual conversations. It provides a comprehensive and accurate account of your loved one's life journey.

Start the interview with the time, location, and names of those present. Use a recording device and/or a transcription app to capture the conversation.

Ensure that the environment is quiet to minimize background noise. Be sure to review your final transcription to fix any accidental errors. If you include handwritten letters in the history, you should also transcribe them.

Keep in mind: Cursive is no longer taught in schools. Those twenty years of age and younger have difficulty reading cursive handwriting.

Simultaneously take notes during the interview. Jot down key points, emotions expressed, and any significant details. This will serve as a quick reference.

Frame questions clearly and encourage detailed responses. If needed, add clarification or more details to ensure a comprehensive understanding.

After the interview, use transcription software or services to convert the recorded audio into text. This will speed up the process and provide an accurate written record.

If you plan to document stories by hand, be sure to do this immediately following the interview, so the information is fresh in your mind.

Organize the transcribed content into categories such as early life, family, challenges, achievements, etc. This helps in creating a structured document. Include relevant context to provide a holistic understanding. This could involve explaining historical events, family relationships, or cultural background.

If possible, keep a copy of the original recording along with the transcribed document for authenticity. Attribute these stories to your interviewee to create an accurate and reliable record.

If more than one person is interviewed, note what information they have provided and their relation to the storyteller.

Share the documented information with family members and store it securely. Consider creating digital and physical copies for safekeeping.

If ongoing interviews are planned, regularly update and expand the documentation to ensure a comprehensive family history.

Allow your interviewee to read your interview before you publish. This is a nice courtesy, and the manuscript may bring up new memories or help them clarify details from the first interview.

By combining recording technology, note-taking, and thoughtful organization, you can create a well-documented and rich account of your elderly family members' experiences and stories.

<u>Notes to Self:</u>

Chapter 23

Follow-Up Questions

Follow-up questions are crucial in interviewing elderly family members because they deepen the conversation and help capture a more comprehensive understanding of their life experiences.

These questions show genuine interest, allowing for richer narratives and a more profound connection.

This is an opportunity to explore emotions, details, and perspectives that might be overlooked with only initial inquiries. Make sure to clarify statements. Often, older people try to remember names and places, and it is your job to double-check with them later or someone else who would know.

If a particular story piques your interest, follow-up with additional questions such as, "What else can you tell me about when your parents immigrated from Ireland? Did you ever hear what their families did for a living? Were there other family members who did not leave Ireland?"

If you have researched and found more areas to be covered, be sure to share with the person you are interviewing. I have found it most helpful to write a list of questions for all involved.

Mail or email your questions to the subjects and then refer to the questions by number. This gives older family members time to reflect and be ready to share more of their stories.

When wrapping up your interview, don't leave your subject in a sad or grieving mood. Change the atmosphere by asking a leading question that will lead them out of despair and into the future.

I have had success with these questions, for example, "What are you having for lunch today?" or "What is your favorite food?" Always end each interview with, "Is there anything else you want to add?"

By asking for elaboration, you invite elders to share valuable insights, memories, and wisdom. This fosters a deeper appreciation for their personal stories and contributes to the preservation of family history.

<u>Notes to Self:</u>

Chapter 24

Ethical and Legal Considerations

When interviewing elderly family members, there are both ethical and legal considerations to be aware of to ensure the interview process is respectful, responsible, and compliant with relevant laws and regulations.

Obtain informed consent from your elderly family member **before** conducting the interview.

Clearly explain the purpose of the interview, how the information will be used, and any potential risks or benefits.

Respect their right to decline participation or withdraw consent at any time. In addition, respect your loved one's privacy by ensuring that sensitive information shared during the interview remains confidential.

Discuss how the information will be stored, shared, and used, and obtain consent for any recordings or documentation. Adhere to relevant privacy laws and regulations, such as HIPAA (in the United States) or GDPR (in the European Union).

Be mindful of cultural norms, values, and traditions when conducting interviews, especially when discussing sensitive topics or personal experiences. It is important to respect cultural differences and avoid imposing your own biases or assumptions onto the conversation.

Ensure that the interview process is conducted with integrity and empathy, avoiding exploitation or coercion of your elderly family member.

Be transparent about your intentions and motives for conducting the interview and prioritize your interviewee's well-being throughout the process.

Make sure to assess your elder's capacity to provide informed consent and participate in the interview.

If the individual has cognitive impairments or diminished decision-making capacity, take appropriate measures to safeguard their rights and well-being, such as involving a legal guardian or healthcare proxy.

Strive for accuracy and authenticity in capturing your elder's life story and family history. Avoid embellishment or distortion of facts, and clearly distinguish between your family member's recollections and factual information.

Respect their perspective and memory, even if it differs from other accounts.

- **Important Note:** Oral history interviews are subject to libel and slander law. As the interviewer, it is important to be sensitive to possible violations of this law and be prepared to seal a portion of the recording and/or edit the transcript so the name of the person being slandered is not made public.

Respect your elder's boundaries and comfort level during the interview. Avoid probing into sensitive or traumatic topics without their explicit consent and be prepared to redirect the conversation or take breaks if necessary to ensure their emotional well-being.

Familiarize yourself with any legal obligations or requirements related to interviewing elderly family members, such as mandatory reporting laws for suspected abuse or neglect. Ensure compliance with applicable laws and regulations governing research ethics, data protection, and confidentiality.

Maintain accurate and secure documentation of the interview process and any information collected, ensuring that records are stored safely. Also, make sure to obtain consent for the use of any photographs, audio recordings, or written materials associated with the interview.

- **Important Note:** Oral history interviews are subject to U.S. copyright law (1978). The interviewee and interviewer must give written permission for public use of audio/video/transcripts.

While you are free to share your interview with your family members, if you intend to donate any material you collected during your interview to a museum or historical society, you and your interviewee **must both sign a release**.

It is important to collect this documentation in a timely manner. If your elderly member passes away before they have signed a release, there is no way to get consent after the fact.

Standardized release forms are useful. You will need a general release and a separate form permitting restrictions or a time seal. You may adapt a general release form document or consult a lawyer and create your own form. The latter may be advisable if your project has any sensitive aspects.

Above all, respect your elder's autonomy and agency throughout the interview process.

Empower them to control the narrative and share their story on their own terms, while providing support and guidance as needed.

By prioritizing ethical principles and legal considerations, you can conduct interviews with your elderly family members in a manner that is respectful, responsible, and mindful of their rights and dignity.

<u>Notes to Self:</u>

<u>Notes to Self:</u>

Chapter 25

Pitfalls You May Encounter

While gathering family stories is a rewarding endeavor, there are potential pitfalls that you may encounter. It is common to experience stumbling blocks within yourself or with someone involved in the project, and they can occur for a variety of reasons.

Being aware of these challenges can help navigate the process more effectively. The following are several techniques to avoid and overcome potential setbacks throughout your interview process.

Self-Doubt:

Challenge: You feel overwhelmed and exhausted and doubt your ability to finish the project.

Solution: Whatever you get done is enough. If it is one story or joke, that is still a slice of history. You do not need to be perfect or aim for a perfect job.

Selective Memory:

Challenge: Family members may remember events differently or choose to highlight specific aspects, leading to a potentially biased narrative.

Solution: Encourage open dialogue, acknowledge diverse perspectives, and cross-reference stories with multiple family members to gain a complete understanding.

Emotional Sensitivity:

Challenge: Some family stories may be tied to sensitive or painful memories, making it challenging to discuss certain topics openly.

Solution: Approach delicate subjects with empathy and sensitivity. Create a safe and non-judgmental space for individuals to share their experiences at their own pace. Reassure the subject that they will have a final say in what is shared.

Generation Gaps:

Challenge: Differences in values, experiences, and perspectives between generations can lead to misunderstandings or misinterpretations of family stories.

Solution: Foster open communication, actively listen to each generation's viewpoints, and seek to understand the context in which stories unfolded. A good example of this is stories of family in a war zone, about who may have done some unthinkable acts to survive. Another example might be bigoted or racist language that was popular in their time in history. Help them understand you do not stand in judgment, and they should not feel guilty.

Incomplete Narratives:

Challenge: Family stories may need more details, context, or multiple viewpoints, resulting in incomplete narratives. Sometimes, the subject will say, "I don't remember," rather than answer a painful or private question.

Solution: Ask probing questions, consult historical records or documents, and involve multiple family members to gather a more complete picture. You will want to double-check. And always remember that whatever you get is enough! Even just one story or anecdote is a blessing for the family and friends.

Reluctance to Share:

Challenge: Some family members may be hesitant to share certain stories due to privacy concerns, embarrassment, or a desire to protect others.

Solution: Respect individuals' boundaries, emphasize the importance of preserving family history and assure confidentiality when needed.

Feelings of Overwhelm:

Challenge: Your subject may feel overwhelmed by the project and want to quit.

Solution: Reassure them that whatever they feel like sharing will be enough. It does not need to be a book; it can be a small story or narrative around a photo.

Overreliance on Memory:

Challenge: Memory can be fallible, and details may become distorted over time. Relying solely on memory can lead to inaccuracies in the retelling of stories.

Solution: Cross-reference stories with historical records, photos, or other family members to verify details. Recognize that memories can evolve, and the essence of the story may be more important than precise details.

Time Constraints:

Challenge: Busy schedules and time constraints may limit the opportunity to explore and document family stories thoroughly.

Solution: Do not aim for an autobiography; instead, write a series of short anecdotes or essays. If you have given the subject a list of questions, keep them on one theme. This will avoid time wasters and jumping all over the place on different storylines.

Cultural and Linguistic Barriers:

Challenge: Families with diverse cultural backgrounds or language barriers may face challenges in accurately translating and conveying the nuances of stories.

Solution: Understand what they are trying to convey. Please refrain from assuming you know what they are expressing. Encourage multilingual resources, involve bilingual family members, and seek external support to bridge linguistic and cultural gaps.

- **Personal Note:** I once interviewed a family friend who had escaped Vietnam. He told me that he could speak in English, but his thoughts were in his native language. I had to offer extra time for him to translate his thoughts into words.

Recognize and address these potential pitfalls if they arise for you. I am confident you can approach gathering family stories with sensitivity, thoroughness, and a commitment to preserving a rich and accurate family history.

Notes to Self:

Chapter 26

Conclusion: Why are Oral Histories Important?

An oral history interview is a great way to capture the magic of your loved one's past and bridge generational gaps.

These stories, anecdotes, memories, photo explanations, etc., capture the essence of the individual storyteller. They provide a window into the family structure, customs, traditions, and values that flow down through the DNA and teachings of the ancestors.

You may be gathering the stories to help you on your personal journey in life, but this effort is also a treasure to your subject.

Elders want to be remembered.

They want to share their life lessons. They are waiting for someone to ask them about their life. Their memories are swirling in their heads and hearts, awaiting a vehicle to share with the world.

Setting aside time to record a historical interview with your loved one will provide powerful insights into their life and guidance for others.

By focusing on the ordinary experiences of everyday day, future readers or listeners will gain an understanding of their own lives.

Remember the quotation:

> "I like myself better when I'm with you."
> — Mitch Albom, *Tuesdays with Morrie*

Throughout the interview process, remind your loved one that their experiences are valued. If you are willing to listen, your interviewee will likely be thrilled to share their life stories with you.

Not Therapy, but Therapeutic

Even though sharing the stories of trauma or tragedy is not therapy, it is therapeutic. The subject can reframe the memory and find healing by telling a long-held secret to a trusted source in a safe environment.

An oral history creates a dynamic living record of someone by sharing their wisdom and experiences. They offer firsthand accounts that complement written records.

This may seem like it has the potential for a time-consuming project. And that is true.

But you, and you alone, have received the calling for this work. Only some people will keep going. Not everyone will realize the importance of this work. I have confidence in you.

Congratulations! You have the interest, the questions to ask, and the tools to move forward in this journey.

Always keep writing. The generations are waiting for your story.

> — *Judy Helm Wright*
> *Personal Historian/IntuitiveWiseWoman*

<u>Notes to Self:</u>

Chapter 27

Oral History Questions

These oral history questions were compiled from various sources and shared with the Association of Personal Historians and in oral history workshops. They are in no particular order or "chunks of time."

You are invited to review this long list with a highlighter and decide which questions will be appropriate for your project. Remember always to ask open-ended questions and listen with an open heart and a desire to capture the stories.

I mentioned the *"Where Generations Meet: A Jar of Questions"* that my granddaughters made for me one year ago. These are great examples of questions to put in your jar or box. Plan on drawing one or two questions out and sharing stories at the dinner table, a sleepover, or whenever the mood strikes you!

You are doing important work, and our team salutes and thanks you.

- What is your full name, and why were you named it?

- Were you named after somebody else?

- Did you have a nickname as you were growing up?

- If you did, what was it, and why did they call you that?

- Have you had other nicknames as an adult?

- What do family members call you now?

- Where were you born, and when?

- Do you remember hearing your grandparents describe their lives? What did they say?

- Do you remember your great-grandparents? What do you know about them?

- Who was the oldest person you can remember in your family as a child? What do you remember about them?

- Do you remember your family discussing world events and politics?

- Was there a chore that you hated doing as a child?

- What would you consider the most important invention made during your lifetime?

- How is the world different now from what it was like when you were a child?

- What kind of books did you like to read?

- Do you remember having a favorite nursery rhyme or bedtime story?

- Do you remember not having enough food because times were hard for your family?

- What were your favorite toys, and what were they like?

- What scared you as a child?

- What were your favorite childhood games?

- Was there a special tree or creek that you loved?

- What were your schools like?

- How did you get to school?

- What was your favorite subject in school and why?

- What subject in school was the easiest for you?

- What was your least favorite subject in school and why?

- Who was your favorite teacher and why were they special?

- How do your fellow classmates from school remember you the best?

- What school activities and sports did you participate in?

- Did you and your friends have a special place where you liked to hang out? If so, where was it, and what did you do there?

- Were you given any special awards for your studies or school activities?

- How many years of education have you completed?

- Do you have a college degree? If so, what was your field of study?

- Did you get good grades?

- Did you like school?

- What did you like the most and least about it?

- What did you usually wear to school? Describe it.

- Were there any fads during your youth that you remember vividly?

- How old were you when you first started dating?

- Do you remember your first date? Describe the circumstances.

- Name a good friend that you have known for the longest period of time. How many years have you been friends?

- Has there been anyone in your life that you would consider to be your kindred spirit or soulmate?

- If so, who were they, and why did you feel a special bond with them?

- How did you meet the person who you would later marry? Describe them.

- Do you remember where you went on the first date with your spouse?

- How long did you know them before you got married?

- Describe your wedding proposal.

- When and where did you get married?

- Describe your wedding ceremony. Who was there?

- Did you have a honeymoon? If so, where did you go?

- How would you describe your spouse? What do (did) you admire about them most?

- How long have you been married (or were you married)?

- What wise advice would you give to a grandchild on their wedding day?

- How did you find out that you were going to be a parent for the first time?

- How many children have you had all together?

- What were their names, birthdates, and birthplaces?

- Do you remember anything that your children did when they were small that really amazed you?

- What is one of the most unusual things that one of your children did regularly when they were small?

- What was the funniest thing you can remember that one of your children said or did?

- If you had to do it all over again, would you change the way you raised your family? How?

- What did you find most difficult about raising children?

- What did you find most rewarding about being a parent?

- Did you spoil any of your children? How?

- Were you a strict or lenient parent?

- Did you find that you had to treat each of your children differently? If so, why?

- How did you first hear that you were a grandparent, and how did you feel about it?

- What advice do you have for your children and grandchildren?

- As a child, what did you want to be when you grew up?

- What was your first job?

- What kind of jobs have you had?

- How did you decide on your career?

- Did you make enough money to live comfortably?

- How long did you have to work each day at your job?

- How old were you when you retired?

- What were the hardest choices that you ever had to make? Do you feel like you made the right choices?

- Who was the person who had the most positive influence in your life? Who were they, and what did they do?

- Do you remember someone saying something to you that greatly impacted how you lived your life? What was it?

- How would you describe yourself politically?

- Are you conservative or liberal, and why?

- What wars took place in your lifetime? How did you feel about them?

- If you served in the military, when and where did you serve, and what were your duties?

- Were you injured in the line of duty if you served in the military? What were the circumstances, and what were your injuries?

- What U.S. president have you admired the most and why?

- As you see it, what are the biggest problems that face our nation, and how do you think they could be solved?

- How tall are you?

- What color was your hair as a young child and then as an adult?

- What color are your eyes?

- Where have you lived as an adult? List the places and the years you lived there.

- Why are you living where you are today?

- Do you wish you had lived somewhere else (If so, where would it be?)?

- Describe your general health.

- What major illnesses or health problems do you remember having?

- Do you have any health problems that are considered hereditary in nature? If so, what are they?

- What do you regularly do for exercise?

- Do you have any bad habits now or in the past? What are they?

- Have you ever been a victim of a crime? What happened?

- Have you ever been a serious accident?

- Has anyone saved your life? Describe.

- Have you ever saved anyone else's life? Describe.

- Have you ever been hospitalized? If so, what for?

- Have you ever had surgery? If so, what for?

- If you could change something about yourself, what would it be?

- Have you ever had an experience that you would consider to be supernatural or psychic? Did you ever know something was going to happen before it did? What was it?

- What do you usually dream about?

- What church, if any, do you attend regularly?

- Describe your religious beliefs.

- Do you believe in an afterlife?

- What was the most stressful experience that you have ever lived through? What helped you get through it?

- What is the scariest thing that has happened to you personally?

- What kind of musical instrument(s) have you learned to play?

- Would you consider yourself to be creative?

- What things have you created that others enjoy?

- How would you describe your sense of humor?

- What is the funniest practical joke that you have ever played on someone?

- What activities have you especially enjoyed as an adult?

- What are your hobbies?

- What do you like to do when you are not working?

- What is the most amazing thing that has ever happened to you?

- What is the most embarrassing thing that has ever happened to you?

- Have you ever met any famous people? Describe what happened.

- What organizations and groups have you belonged to?

- Have you ever won any special awards or prizes as an adult? What were they for?

- Describe a time and place when you remember feeling truly at peace and happy to be alive. Where were you, and what were you doing?

- What is the most beautiful place you have ever visited, and what was it like?

- What was the longest trip you have ever been on? Where did you go?

- What has been your favorite vacation? Where did you go, and why was it special?

- What was your favorite place you have ever been to, and what was it like?

- What pets have you had?

- Do you have a favorite story about a pet? What is it?

- Is there anything you have always wanted to do but haven't?

- What is your favorite style of music?

- What is your favorite musical instrument?

- Who is your favorite musical group?

- What is your favorite song?

- Who is your favorite singer?

- Who is your favorite movie star?

- What is your favorite movie?

- Who is your favorite artist?

- What is your favorite painting?

- What is your favorite poet?

- What is your favorite poem?

- What is your favorite TV program?

- Who is your favorite author?

- What is your favorite book?

- What is your favorite season?

- What is your favorite tree?

- What is your favorite flower?

- What is your favorite holiday?

- What is your favorite color?

- What is your favorite sport?

- Who Is your favorite athlete?

- What is your favorite animal?

- What is your favorite meal?

- What is your favorite fruit?

- What is your favorite vegetable?

- What is your favorite candy?

- What is your favorite cookie?

- What is your favorite drink?

- What is your favorite restaurant?

- What is your favorite flavor of ice cream?

- What is your favorite board game?

- What is your favorite card game?

  - **Personal note:** My favorite questions are: "What would you like to tell your grandchildren?" and "How would you like to be remembered?"

Notes to Self:

Judy Helm Wright:
Who I Am & Why You Should Trust Me

Hello! Welcome to this exciting journey of sharing your wisdom and capturing family stories for your children's children and those who will benefit from your efforts. My name is Judy Helm Wright — Author/Personal Historian/IntuitiveWiseWoman.

I often share about the honor of being named "Auntie Artichoke — a wise woman who loves unconditionally" by Indigenous tribes I worked with in Hawaii and Montana.

As a founding member of the Association of Personal Historians and the Montana Story Keepers, I was part of a valuable gathering of people committed to the importance of storytelling.

I have taught memoir writing for twenty-five years in many communities. What I knew then about how memory works and what research and life experiences have taught me now is vastly different. As we explore this exciting calling, you too will benefit from this research and knowledge.

The journey to find and share your stories will be some of the most important work you will do. Stories create connection, and human connection enriches your life.

You will be guided, not just by me as a Personal Historian, but by your ancestors and those who have influenced your life in meaningful ways. Think of Mitch Albom and *Tuesdays with Morrie* and how that small book has impacted not only family and friends but the entire world.

Know that your story will be treasured and loved by those who read, view, and hear your wisdom.

Please join us for additional educational workshops, online courses, and resources at https://www.MemoirLifeStoryWriting.com.

PS: Your satisfaction and feedback are invaluable. If you have had a positive experience with this guide, I would be immensely grateful if you could take a moment to share your thoughts and impressions. Your glowing review not only validates my efforts but also inspires me to continue to bring you helpful writing content. Thank you for your trust and support!

References

Albom, Mitch. 2002. *Tuesdays with Morrie.* Crown: New York.

Rooks, Diane. 2012. *Spinning Gold out of Straw: How Stories Heal.* Self-published, Kindle Direct Publishing.

Stone, Richard. 2004. *Stories-the Family Legacy-A Guide for Recollection and Sharing* Storyworks Publishing, Maitland, Florida.

Vanchieri, Cori. "Q&A: How Music Can Cultivate a Healthy Brain." *AARP.* Last modified January 09, 2024. https://www.aarp.org/health/brain-health/info-2024/neuroscientist-on-music-and-brain-health.html

Wittig Albert, Susan. 1997. *Writing from Life: Telling Your Soul's Story.* Self-published. Kindle Direct Publishing.

Wright, Judy Helm. "What is a Legacy Letter?" *Blazing Trails.56(1).* Last modified January 2024. *https://mycommunityonline.com/publication-page/missoula-senior-citizens-center-association-inc?pid=4a13c464-c45a-4dc8-993e-919e3ffde5ea&type=Community&acc=05-1156,*